Easter

Program Builder No. 29

LILLENAS®
DRAMA

Easter Program Builder No. 29

Creative Resources for Program Directors

Compiled by Kimberly R. Messer

lillenas
PUBLISHING COMPANY

PO Box 419527
Kansas City, MO 64141

Questions? Please write or call:

Lillenas Publishing Company
Drama Resources
P.O. Box 419527
Kansas City, MO 64141
Phone: 816-931-1900 • Fax: 816-412-8390
E-mail: drama@lillenas.com
Web Site: www.lillenasdrama.com

Cover Design by J. R. Caines

Contents

Recitations for Preschool

A Beautiful Day!

What a beautiful day
for me to get to say,
Happy Easter!

Karen Lee

Yay! Yay!

Yay! Yay!
That's what I say.
Let's celebrate this Easter Day!

K. R. Messer

Life in Christ

Christ came to earth
To end its strife,
And be for us
A symbol of life.

Dorothy Heibel

Jesus Came Out of the Tomb

No more death
No more gloom.
Jesus came out of the tomb.
Sunny skies
Beautiful flowers.
Let us celebrate God's power.

K. R. Messer

Hallelujah! He Has Risen!

ALL: Christ is risen! Christ is risen!
CHILD 1: Let's celebrate the day.
ALL: Christ is risen! Christ is risen!
CHILD 2: It's time to sing and pray.
ALL: Hallelujah! Hallelujah!
CHILD 3: He's Lord and God and King!
ALL: Hallelujah! Hallelujah!
CHILD 4: He rules over everything!

Margaret Primrose

Easter Greeting

On this very special day,
And in my own special way,
I am very pleased to say,
Happy Easter!

Karen Lee

Jesus Rocks

Jesus rocks!
I'll tell you why.
He told 'ol Death to go "bye bye."
Left the tomb in victory.
Forever saving you and me.

K. R. Messer

Ten Little Lambs

CHILD 1: Ten little lambs all look
the same,
Everyone has a
different name.

CHILD 2: Nine little lambs with
different faces,
Everyone from
different places.

CHILD 3: Eight little lambs do not
speak the same,
For everyone a Savior
came.

CHILD 4: Seven little lambs some
short, some tall,
Learn in church God
loves them all.

CHILD 5: Six little lambs running
to and fro,
Measure our height,
watch us grow.

CHILD 6: Five little lambs at an
altar kneel,
Serving Jesus is very
real.

CHILD 7: Four little lambs want
to sing,
Praises to the only
King.

CHILD 8: Three little lambs all
smiling bright,
Jesus came on
Christmas night.

CHILD 9: Two little lambs loving
each other,
Share the good news
with one another.

CHILD 10: One little lamb that
carries our sin
Jesus the One who
helps us win.

Robert E. Snodgrass

Thanks for Coming

We're glad you smile when we sing
And clap for each poem we say.
We're happy that you're with us
On this very special day.
Thank you. *(optional)*

Margaret Primrose

Recitations for Ages 5 to 7

My Savior and Friend

Jesus is my Savior;
Jesus is my Friend.
He came to bring me life—
Life that will never end.

He forgave me of my sins.
Now I'm happy and free,
And I can live with Him
For all eternity.

Margaret Primrose

An Easter Prayer

To the Lord in Heaven above,
Thank You for Your gift of love.
Thank You for Your Son who died
To save us from our sinful pride.
And thank You, Lord, for Mom and Dad.
They love me too, and make me glad.
Bless us now as we partake
And on this Easter, celebrate!

Karen Lee

Let's Sing and Praise Jesus

Jesus died for you and me;
Jesus died to set us free.
Now and forever let us sing
Praises to our Lord and King!

Margaret Primrose

He's Coming Again

CHILD 1: "Father, forgive them,"
Jesus cried
When He hung on the cross
And suffered and died.

CHILD 2: He gave His life
For you and me;
Forgave our sins,
And set us free.

CHILD 3: He's coming again;
It may be soon;
It may be morning
Or night or noon.

CHILD 4: We'll rise to meet Him
In His home in the sky
Where we'll live with Him
And never, ever die.

Margaret Primrose

Recitations for Ages 8 to 10

Willing to Die

CHILD 1: Though Jesus healed the sick
And made the blind to see,
He hung on a rugged old cross
That was made from an ugly tree.

CHILD 2: He endured the jeers of the crowd
And the nails in His hands and feet.
He wore a crown of thorns
Without any thought of defeat.

CHILD 3: Jesus was willing to die
For the worst of sinful men.
He knew He would conquer death,
And He knew He would live again.

ALL: Alleluia!

Margaret Primrose

I'm Glad

I'm glad I know the story
Of Jesus' lowly birth.
I'm glad He died for me
And for everyone on earth.
I'm glad He rose again
And never again will die.
I'm glad I'll see Him some day
And live with Him in the sky.

Margaret Primrose

The Victor

Christ's tomb was like an egg
That became an empty shell,
For Jesus is the Victor
Over sin and death and hell.

No guarded grave could hold Him;
He never again will die,
And if we trust Him as Savior,
We'll live with Him in the sky.

Margaret Primrose

My Easter Offering

My daddy wrote a check
To bring to church today.
It's a special Easter offering
For people far away
Who have never heard of Jesus
And don't know how to pray.
I have a piggy bank
So I brought my offering too.
I pray the Lord will bless
The little that I do
To share the Easter story
With children like me and you.

Margaret Primrose

My Easter Prayer

Mother curled my hair
And shopped for the dress I wear.
Daddy dressed my brother
And set him in his chair.

Grandma helped me write
The poem I plan to say.
I think we're almost ready
To go to church today.

I'm glad that what I'll say
Is more than just a part.
I'm glad that it's a prayer
That comes from deep in my
heart.

(With bowed head)

Thank You, thank You, Jesus,
For this happy Easter day.
Thank You that You love us
And hear us when we pray.

Thank You that You died
To save us from our sin.
Thank You that You rose
And will never die again.

Margaret Primrose

He Is King

By Margaret Primrose

Though Jesus came as Lord of all,
He slept in a manger in a cattle stall.
He grew up in a little-known town
And had no palace, no throne, no crown.

He discipled some fishermen of Galilee
Who would spread His word from sea to sea.
He healed the sick and raised the dead,
But in spite of His love, He suffered and bled.

"Father, forgive them," the Savior prayed
For those who condemned Him, and those who strayed.
He felt the nails in His hands and feet
But suffered and died without defeat.

His borrowed tomb was guarded and sealed.
It couldn't hold Him, His keepers revealed.
He appeared to those who were willing to believe
That by coming to Him, new life they'd receive.

He will reign in our hearts and forever will be
The Lord of the earth of the sky and the sea.
He'll take us to heaven to live with Him there
In the beautiful mansions He has gone to prepare.

Easter Sunrise

By Beth Westcott

Cast:

Mary Magdalene

(Mary Magdalene, *speaking to people in congregation as she walks down the aisle. She may be in costume or not.)*

Mary Magdalene: Do you know what happened?

Do you know where He is?

(From the front)

We came to the tomb this morning—early, the sun was just up. We brought our burial spices to place around His body.

"What will we do with the stone?" we wondered. "Will the soldiers let us in?"

But . . . there were no soldiers! And the stone was rolled away from the entrance! And the tomb . . . the tomb was empty!

How could this be?

Where was His body?

Then the angels appeared—great shining ones, frightening us out of our wits!

"Why seek ye the living among the dead?" they asked. "He is not here, for He is risen as He said." (KJV)

We raced back to Jerusalem to find Jesus' closest friends who were in hiding for fear and sorrow.

"The tomb is empty! The Lord's body is gone! The angels told us He is risen!"

Huh—they thought us to be crazy women.

But I . . . I saw Him with my own eyes. He spoke to me! Our Lord is risen indeed!

(Exit)

On the Way to Emmaus

By Margaret Primrose

My friend and I were trudging
To our little country town
And hoping to arrive
Before the sun went down.

We had both believed in Jesus—
He'd become our dearest friend—
But we'd heard the jeering crowd
When our Master was condemned.

He'd hung on a rugged cross
While He wore a crown of thorns.
His enemies had triumphed;
We could only mourn.

This morning, very early,
His guarded tomb was bare.
Though some women claimed He'd risen,
It left us in despair.

When a stranger came to join us,
He shared with us God's word.
He repeated many things
We had really never heard.

When at last we reached our village,
We begged our friend to stay.
Our hearts were burning within us
Because of what we heard Him say.

When He sat to eat with us,
He broke and blessed the bread.
In a moment we knew 'twas Jesus—
He'd risen from the dead.

All at once He vanished,
   And we knew what we should do.
We hurried to the city
   To share our story too.

As we began, He stood in our midst
   And told us not to fear.
We could touch His hands and feet
   And know that He was near.

He told us to stay in Jerusalem
   For power from above,
Then go to tell all nations
   Of His everlasting love.

EASTER MORNING MEDITATION

By Virginia M. Merritt

I awaken. I wink one eyelid. Night has lightened. Dawn is near.

I roll over and remember: women weeping. Women worrying. Women wondering as they gather myrrh and aloes in soft bundles, pulling shawls around their shoulders, closing wooden doors behind them, walking down the quiet alleys, meeting at the outer wall.

Whispering, they walk on, drawn together in their duty, locked together in their love.

Treading twig and thistle, dewy grass, and stone and sand, they pull shawls a little closer, hugging bundles closer yet. Their fear and sadness mingle . . . but what is this? There is no guard. The rock's rolled back. There is no body. He is gone. He is gone!

Bundles abandoned, duty forsaken, shawls freely flying, the women turn. Oh! Hallelujah! Christ is risen! Just as He said: He's risen indeed!

I arise and rejoice. I stretch and celebrate the day. No somber black awaits my dressing. Purple and teal will tell my joy. Festal foods and pealing bells, happy hugs and banners waved, children's voices raised in song, robins hopping in the yard.

All is changed. All is new. There is life and hope and grace.

The sun is up and I am too

Christ is risen. He's risen indeed.

Easter Promises

By Margaret Primrose

Scripture References: Isaiah 1:18; John 1:12; 3:16; 11:25; 14:2-3; Acts 16:31; Romans 5:8; 10:9; 10:11; 10:13; 2 Corinthians 5:17; 1 Timothy 2:5; 1 John 1:9; Revelation 3:20

Cast:

RACHEL
MRS. MILLER
BOYS and GIRLS—There are 14 verses suggested, but use as many as you have people in the class

(RACHEL *enters the classroom where the others are already gathered. She addresses* MRS. MILLER.)

RACHEL: Good morning, Mrs. Miller. Happy Easter.

MRS. MILLER: Happy Easter to you too.

RACHEL: I brought something for you and for each of the boys and girls in our class.

MRS. MILLER: Oh, it's a basket of Easter eggs.

RACHEL: Yes, but these plastic eggs don't just have candy in them. Grandma and I put something special in them.

MRS. MILLER: Good! We like surprises, don't we?

ALL: Yes. Of course. *(Continue with similar responses.)*

(RACHEL *gives each class member a plastic egg. The eggs may contain a chocolate kiss as well as a Bible verse.)*

MRS. MILLER: Oh, you've put a Bible verse in this egg.

RACHEL: There's a different one in each egg.

MRS. MILLER: Let's read them. I'll begin.

(Each person reads the verse in their Easter egg.)

MRS. MILLER: Thank you, Rachel. *(Turns to class)* It sounds as if we have a lot to talk about this morning, doesn't it?

RISE UP!

An Easter Drama—Sola Gloria Dei

By Russ Reemtsma

Cast:

ANGELA WILKINS—Single mother who is proud to have risen up out of poverty
TERRI FRANKLIN—Angela's best friend
SOPHIE WILKINS—Angela's daughter
SKIP WILKINS—Angela's brother who gets in trouble with the law
FLOYD CARSON—Inmate who shares a cell with Skip. Floyd is mentally handicapped, but loves Jesus
MELISSA MCBAIN—Sophie's best friend
AMBER MCBAIN—Melissa's mother
MAXINE LEAVY—Sophie's Sunday School teacher
PRISCILLA BRAMBLE—Angela's nosy, interfering neighbor; loves to gossip
PASTOR ROGER BARNES—Pastor of the church where Sophie attends

Production Note: Suggested music (*) information is noted at the end of the script.

***Choir Opening:** "Arise! Arise!"

Prologue

SKIP *(looking out at audience):* Oh, hello. I wasn't expecting to meet *you* here. Whatcha been up to? *(Pauses, as if talking to a friend)* Me? I'm out on an errand for my sister, Angela. I'm looking for a new Bible for her daughter, Sophie. *(Pause)* You don't know *Angela*? Oh, I thought everybody around here knew her. *(Pause)* Why's that? Well, if you've lived any time around here you would have heard about Angie. She's one of those, you know—driven people, a real "rags-to-riches," "welfare-to-millionaire" person. *(Pause)* Yep, I really did say "*millionaire.*" *(Pause)* Say what? You really wanna know about how that happened? Well, there's a lot to the story. OK, I've got a few minutes. I'll tell you, if you don't rush me.

Ever since Angela was a little girl she had ambition, you know . . . a real get-ahead drive. She always had an agenda. As for me, my agenda always landed me, well . . . in the dunce corner, the principal's office and other places of punishment. I always used to say luck wasn't on my side, but now I know better . . . Angela always used to scold me and tease me. She'd say, "Hey, brother, do you know why your name is 'Skip'? Because when they were passing out talent and brains, you got skipped!" And later on she would say my name was 'Skip' because I'd skip around from job to job. Or I'd skip in and out of jail. Yeah, I've made my share of trouble throughout my life, but as hard as Angela could be, she was the one who'd get me out of it with her ruthless determination and quick wits. Even though we had very little money growing up, we had each other. *(Chuckles)*

Determination . . . Angie had a little phrase that she said constantly throughout her life. She'd say, "*Someday, I'm going to rise up out of this . . .*" She proved that to be true several times. That was especially true when her husband, Tom, left her when Sophie, their daughter, was only eighteen months old. Angela was now a single mom on welfare. That lasted about three years until she got her Bachelor's degree. That's right . . . a four-year degree in three. But her motto of *rising up* drove her to success. That's why she had little compassion for anyone else who had any weakness or limitations. She figured if she could get ahead, anybody could. She didn't need anybody. She didn't have any time for God or religion. She did send Sophie to Pastor Roger Barnes' church daycare. That was the cheapest childcare she could find while she went to school. Over the years, Sophie attended the Sunday School and was a regular church attendee. Angie went on from promotion to promotion and had little time for God and little patience for any kind of "God talk." She was too busy in her profession. She'd keep saying "*Someday, I'm going to rise. To the top.*" She really had the world by the tail and *was* rising until an unlikely little guy named Floyd showed her what "rising up" is all about. *(*SKIP *chuckles, then breaks out into all out laughter.)*

Scene 1

Setting: Angela's home

*(*ANGELA *is seated in the living room.* SOPHIE *is standing next to her, clearly agitated.)*

SOPHIE: Mommy, I'm gonna be late for Sunday School. Can you hurry? Puh-lease? I've been late the last three Sundays!

ANGELA *(phone to her ear):* Hold on, baby, I just have one more call to make. Terri? Hey! How's it going? How's your day look? I finally closed on the deal last night. Yeah, the Growgan account. Can you believe it? I've been working on it for six months and finally landed it. I'm ready to celebrate! How about a fancy dinner and a movie? My treat! *(Pause)* What? *(Chuckles)* Well, let's just say I can afford to be a big spender, for a *long* time. *(Pauses)* OK, I've got to drop Sophie off at church and I'll pick you up in an hour. Yeah, me too. Bye.

SOPHIE: Hey, you promised you'd come to church with me. You can't go out with Terri.

ANGELA: I'm sorry, hon, but I've worked so hard on this account, I just need a break. Look, Easter is three weeks away. I *promise* I'll come on Easter Sunday. OK? But we have to get you out the door. *Now*!

*(*ANGELA *and* SOPHIE *prepare to leave.)*

SOPHIE *(walking toward the door):* Do you really mean it, Mom? My Sunday School class is going to be singing in church on Easter morning. I really hope you mean it. We're gonna sing the song "We Welcome Glad Easter."

ANGELA: Of course, I mean it. When I say I'm going to be there, I will. In the business world, when you say you're going to do something, you do it. That's the only way you get to the top. *(To herself.)* Someday, I'm going to rise up—

SOPHIE *(disappointed):* I know, Mom . . . to the top. Can we go now?

*(*ANGELA *and* SOPHIE *begin to leave when the phone rings.)*

ANGELA *(turns to answer):* Hello?

(Lights up on PRISCILLA BRAMBLE.*)*

PRISCILLA: Hello, Angela-dear. This is Priscilla Bramble, your neighbor. How are you doing?

ANGELA *(rolling her eyes and throwing her arms up):* Oh hello, Priscilla. How can I help you?

PRISCILLA: Well, I'm sure you remember my good friend Florine. She called me this morning and told me she read in the paper that your brother, Skip, is in jail again. So, I just had to run down to Calvin's Market and get myself a paper to see if it was so and, sure enough, it says right here in the Hintsfield Register Gazette: "Skip Wilkins apprehended for DUI." *(Sarcastically)* What's DUI, sweetie?

ANGELA *(irritated, feigning being secretive):* Priscilla, don't tell anybody, but DUI stands for "Doing Undercover Investigation." I'm sure that

Skip is doing his part to help the police. *(Sweetly)* But thank you so much for keeping a close eye on my family. That's so sweet *(said through clenched teeth)* of you!

PRISCILLA: Oh, don't mention it, dearie. I'm just doing my Christian duty. Goodbye. *(Hangs up)*

ANGELA *(mocking* PRISCILLA, *grimacing):* "I'm just doing my Christian duty, dearie. Goodbye." *Good riddance!*

SOPHIE: Come on, Mom, let's *go! (Exit)*

Scene 2

Setting: A holding cell at Hintsfield County jail

*(*PASTOR BARNES *is praying with* FLOYD, *Bible in hand.* SKIP *is sitting nearby, not paying attention.)*

PASTOR BARNES: . . . and Lord, thank you that Ol' Floyd knows you and has the hope of your resurrection. Give him peace as he is here in this place. I pray for his health, too, Lord, as it has been declining lately. In our Savior's name, Amen.

FLOYD *(coughing):* Amen! Floyd thanks his pastor for coming. Floyd is happy.

PASTOR BARNES: Thank *you,* Floyd. You make me happy too. I hope that you're able to get out of jail pretty soon.

FLOYD: Floyd is happy in jail too! Pastor should not worry. Not worry—no! Floyd thanks the pastor for praying for Floyd. Floyd is happy.

PASTOR BARNES: Well, goodbye, brother Floyd. I'll see you next week. *(Places hand on* FLOYD'S *shoulder.)*

FLOYD: OK, OK. Next week. Bye-bye, Pastor Roger. *(Waving)*

*(*PASTOR BARNES *turns to go and sees* SKIP WILKINS, *who is busy minding his own business.)*

PASTOR BARNES: Hello, I'm Roger Barnes. *(Goes over to* SKIP, *extending his hand.)*

SKIP *(sitting, not looking up):* OK, so you're the pastor. Look, I really don't wanna talk, OK? *(Sarcastically)* If I want religion, I'll talk to Pretty Boy Floyd here.

PASTOR BARNES: Hey, *(good naturedly chuckles)* I can take a hint. But don't sell our friend Floyd short. He's got a handle on life that others don't have. Look, let me just leave you a Bible and I'm outta here. *(Lays it by* SKIP *and leaves.)*

FLOYD: There goes Floyd's pastor. Pastor is a nice man. Pastor tells the truth. *(Coughs)* Pastor tells about Jesus going away. Floyd is happy that Jesus got up and goes away.

SKIP *(to himself):* I'm not sure what's worse— *(shaking his head)* this hangover or getting stuck with the village idiot!

FLOYD: Jesus gets up. He goes out and goes away. *(Coughs)*

SKIP: I wish *you'd* get out and go away.

FLOYD: Me too. Floyd does not like jail. Floyd does not like jail people. You are not nice. Pastor Roger is nice, not you.

SKIP *(regretful):* Look, Floyd, Skip is—I mean—*I* am sorry. I don't want to be mean. I'm just very angry that I did something very bad, very stupid.

FLOYD: Oh! Stupid! People call Floyd stupid. But Floyd is not. *(Coughs)* Floyd loves Jesus and Jesus loves Floyd. Floyd is happy, not stupid. Are you happy? Or stupid?

SKIP: I'd have to say I'm more stupid than happy right now.

FLOYD: Skip can read, yeah? Look what Pastor Roger gives Floyd—a book. Floyd's book has pictures of Jesus! *(Hands it to* SKIP.*)* Read to Floyd, please. Read. *(Smiles and coughs)*

SKIP: Well, OK, since you said, "Please." *(Looks at book)* I'll be—a children's book. It's religious . . .

FLOYD *(pointing to the book):* Read, man. Read to Floyd.

SKIP: Now, don't go getting bossy like Angela. I'll read. Let's see . . . Here's a picture . . . it says . . . Jesus carries His cross to Gol—Golg—Golga—

FLOYD: Golgotha! That's a bad hillside. Bad people killed Jesus. Very bad!

SKIP: Yes. There are a lot of mean looking people around Jesus. Very bad, as you say.

FLOYD: No! *We* are the bad people who killed Jesus! Floyd and Skip.

SKIP: What are you talking about? This picture is not *us.* These are the *bad* people.

FLOYD: Nope, nope! *(Coughs)* Sins put Jesus there. *You* did, Skip.

SKIP: What do you mean, Floyd? *(To himself.)* What do I mean? Why am I talking to this wifty guy? I may as well be talking to a mailbox.

FLOYD: No! You are not very nice. You put Jesus on that cross. *(Points to picture in the book)* So did Floyd. But he is happy now, Floyd is. Yes, he is very happy. Jesus' cross is Floyd's cross. Jesus' cross is Skip's cross too. Is Skip happy? Or stupid?

SKIP: Go take a nap, Floyd.

***Choir:** "At the Cross"

Scene 3

Setting: Dinner at a nice restaurant

*(*ANGELA *and* TERRI *are seated at a table eating dinner.)*

TERRI: I didn't want to bring this up, Angie, but I saw the paper today and—

ANGELA: Yeah, don't tell me anymore. My wonderful Christian neighbor told me all about it. And that *loser* brother of mine. That boy never listened! I could just wring his neck.

TERRI: Maybe you shouldn't keep bailing him out of trouble.

ANGELA *(clearly angry):* Let's not go there, Terri. He's still my brother.

TERRI: Sounds like he's more of a *bother* than a brother. Why don't you let him sit a few days before you jail him out? Maybe some time there would do him good.

ANGELA: You know, Terri, maybe you're right. I think I'll let ol' loser boy sit in the Hintsfield County tank for a while. Why not? Maybe he'll think about how to *rise up* out of this mess. I can't be too worried about him while I'm rising to the top.

TERRI: You got it, girl. Go for the top. Rise up and shine!

ANGELA: Say, Ter', I have kind of a, well . . . favor to ask.

TERRI: Sure, hon, what do you need?

ANGELA: Sophie asked me to come to her Easter service. She's singing. I promised that I'd go to the service and I haven't been to a church since I was a little girl. Would you mind going with me?

TERRI: Mind? Not at all. My folks are going to be in Florida, so I'm free. I will probably be just as scared as you. I'm not used to church people.

ANGELA: Yeah. Church people scare me. Can you imagine a congregation full of people like my neighbor, *"Saint Priscilla"*?

TERRI: Definitely not your "get-ahead person."

ANGELA *(sarcastically):* She's just a busybody doing her Christian duty . . . ratting on everybody!

Scene 4

Setting: Priscilla on the phone

PRISCILLA: Oh, Florine! You wouldn't believe it! It was wonderful. I asked her what DUI meant. Can you believe it? Yeah. You know what she told me? She said, "Doing Undercover Investigations." *(Laughs)* What does she take me for?

(Pauses and listens)

What's that? *(Pause)* I know! She's driving a new car these days. Seems like she gets one every couple of years. And you know what? She lets the church bus come and get poor Sophie every week while she sleeps in. I don't know, Flo'. What's this world coming to?

Scene 5

Setting: At church; getting ready for the children's anthem

*(*SOPHIE, MELISSA, *and several children talking and giggling)*

PASTOR BARNES: OK, everyone. Let's get to work.

(Children ignore the instruction.)

PASTOR BARNES *(clapping hands):* Come on, now. Let's get serious.

MOLLY: Pastor Roger, what does "serious" mean?

CORRINA: I know! It has something to do with a mule.

MOLLY: Why's that?

CORRINA: Well, I heard Mrs. Pederson say that when Pastor Roger directs our choir he looks as serious as an old mule.

(Children giggle.)

PASTOR BARNES: Let's calm down now.

CORRINA: What? What did I say? I'm sorry, Pastor!

PASTOR BARNES: OK, that's enough of that. Let's sing our song.

***Children's Choir:** "We Welcome Glad Easter"

Scene 6

Setting: In back room, following choir number

(All children have left except SOPHIE *and* MELISSA *who stand talking.)*

MELISSA: I'm so sorry about your mom, Sophie. I'll pray for her.

SOPHIE: Ya know what, Missy? My mom is a good mom! She takes good care of me, but she just doesn't know—you know what I mean?

MELISSA: Yeah. I'll get my mom to pray for her too. Maybe she and your mom can get together sometime.

SOPHIE: I'm not sure about that. She won't talk to *anybody* who lives in the old neighborhood anymore. She keeps saying *(singsong voice)* "I'm rising up! I'm going to the top!" It seems like she's too good for anybody who doesn't have money.

MELISSA: Oh. *(Embarrassed)*

SOPHIE: I am so sorry, Missy! I didn't mean to make you feel bad. You're my best friend. We've been friends since we were little. I didn't mean—

MELISSA: I know what you meant. I think your mom is just covering up a lot of hurt by making a lot of money. When I think about my mom and me, well, I get happy since we both came to know Jesus. That's something money can never buy!

SOPHIE: Yeah. Hey, just pray for my mom, OK?

MELISSA: Sure thing.

Scene 7

Setting: Same as at the beginning

(Looks at his friend—the audience.)

SKIP: You know, it's hard to admit, but my boy Floyd was starting to get to me. As the days passed, he would just spill out all kinds of Jesus stuff. Some of it made sense, and some of it just seemed to incoherently spill out of poor Floyd's simple mind. I ignored all the nonsense. But it was the stuff that made sense that really bothered me. I couldn't help but start to put the pieces together. It was very simple to understand, but very hard to admit. I remember this one conversation—if you want to call it a conversation—with my somewhat disengaged evangelist . . .

Scene 8

Setting: In the jail

*(*SKIP *is sitting on the bunk, looking miserable.* FLOYD *is pacing.)*

FLOYD: Skip is not happy. Skip is stupid. Skip is not happy. Skip is stup—

SKIP *(angrily breaks in):* Would you *shut* your mouth?

FLOYD: Don't Skip remember? Skip said that he is stupid, not Floyd—

SKIP: I said I did a stupid thing! *(To himself.)* How did I ever get stuck with this, this—

FLOYD: Be gentle on ol' Floyd. Skip is carrying a load. Skip is not stupid, but Skip is not happy, neither. Floyd is happy, though.

SKIP *(letting up a little, runs his hand through his hair):* Floyd, what reason do either you or I have to be happy? We're in jail, man! We're unemployed. We've got a record. Don't' you understand? How are we ever going to rise up out of this mess?

FLOYD *(beaming):* Rise up? Yes! Ol' Floyd's a *risin' up! (Looks up)* Yes, Jesus! Floyd's ready! When? Floyd is ready *now!*

SKIP *(appalled):* Floyd, what do you mean?

*(*SKIP *turns to audience resuming his storytelling; set aside within the scene.)*

SKIP: I couldn't get a straight answer out of Floyd that night, but I knew he clearly understood something I desperately wished I could come close to understanding. Floyd's hope was not a storybook wish. His world was *real,* not *fantasy.* Then one day when Pastor Barnes was ready to leave from visiting Floyd . . .

*(*SKIP *returns to scene, joining* FLOYD *and* PASTOR BARNES *in jail.)*

PASTOR BARNES *(preparing to leave):* Well, see ya, Floyd. We'll try to find someplace for you—

FLOYD: Okie, dokie, Preacher. Love you, man!

SKIP *(sitting on cot, stands and walks toward* PASTOR*):* Pastor Barnes—

PASTOR BARNES *(turning around):* Skip? *(Jokingly)* Ah, he does talk. *(Chuckles)*

*(*FLOYD *goes over and sits on cot, reading a book.)*

SKIP *(sheepishly):* Oh, yeah . . . hey . . . I've been pretty rude to you. I'm really sorry about that.

PASTOR BARNES: That's OK, Skip. Forget about it. What's on your mind?

SKIP: Well, I don't know how to put this, but Floyd—

PASTOR BARNES: He kinda gets to ya, doesn't he? I'll bet that you're probably wondering what makes him tick—why he can be so hopeful and assured.

SKIP: Yeah, that's it. I know he's not "all together," *(pointing to his temple with index finger)* ya know? But if this *(holding up the children's book)* can help a guy like him . . . I mean, this guy really should have nothing to hope for. He has no money, no education, no family, no nothing. I want what he has.

PASTOR BARNES: You want to trust Christ to be your Savior.

*(*SKIP *moves CS.)*

SKIP: Right there in prison, I realized that it wasn't all the other "bad" people that put Christ on that cross. I acknowledged that what Jesus did—you know, died and rose again—He did for me, for my sin. I placed all of my faith in Him that day. I didn't all of a sudden "get religion." Pastor Barnes explained to me what Floyd was talking about . . . Jesus "rising up."

I trusted Christ to be my Savior that day . . . And He forgave me of all my sin and changed me . . . forever.

(Exits)

***Choir:** "We Shall See Jesus"

*(*SKIP *reenters to CS.)*

SKIP: Before Pastor Barnes left that day, he asked me a big favor, a huge favor. Floyd and I were set to get out of jail on the same day. Because Floyd had nowhere immediately to go, Pastor Barnes asked if I could find a place for Floyd while the church made arrangements to find a more permanent home. I said, "Sure!" *(Grins)*

Scene 9

Setting: Angela's home

*(*ANGELA *is standing, glaring at* SKIP *who is seated on the couch.)*

ANGELA: No. Absolutely not! Do you think I'm crazy? What were you thinking, loser brother? You want me to have some loser half-witted tramp stay here? I'm doing everything I can not to put you out!

SKIP: Listen, Angie, I know that it's a hard thing to ask, but Pastor Barnes said he would get—

ANGELA *(becoming increasingly strident):* Hard thing? Hard thing? How about *impossible*? You—you—

(Telephone rings)

ANGELA *(composing herself while glaring at* SKIP*):* Hello. Oh hello, Priscilla.

(Lights come up on PRISCILLA.*)*

PRISCILLA: Hello, Angela-dear. How's it going? My offer is still good. I did have a college psychology class you know.

ANGELA: No thank you, Mrs. Bramble. We are perfectly *(clenched teeth)* happy. But thanks just the same. *(Syrupy sweet)* You're *such* a dear.

PRISCILLA: Oh, you know me, sweetie. I'm just doing my Christian duty. *(*ANGELA *mouths this word for word.)* Goodbye.

ANGELA: Goodbye, Priscilla. *(Hangs up)* That woman has the mouth of a—

PRISCILLA *(to the air):* Oh, Flo! You're gonna love this . . . *(starts to dial; lights down)*

*(*SKIP *goes to CS, speaks directly to audience.)*

SKIP: Now, my sister is, or was, impetuous, frank, and rude. But she is not heartless. Yeah. It took a lot of explaining, bribing and, yes, even a little conniving, but we agreed that ol' Floyd could stay with us at Angie's until the day after Easter, then . . . *(mimicking a rocket with his hands)* Phsst—he is outta there!

Scene 10

Setting: Angela's home, one week before Easter Sunday

*(*ANGELA, SKIP, *and* SOPHIE *are in the living room.* FLOYD *enters, holding up his religious children's book, singing off-key over and over the chorus from "Low in the Grave He Lay.")*

FLOYD: Up from the grave He arose! Up from the grave He arose! Up from the grave He arose! Ol' Floyd's gonna *rise*, yes siree, gonna get up just like Jesus. Ol' Floyd's gonna *rise up*!

*(*SOPHIE *plugs her ears while* FLOYD *sings.)*

ANGELA: Skip! Stop him. He's driving me crazy! I don't know if I can handle any more of this. How did I ever let you talk me into this in the first place? You and your loser friends. How did I ever think I could put up with this for a whole week? What will the neighbors think? *(Smacks her head)* Oh boy, I can just imagine what Priscilla Bramble is going to gossip about. This'll be all over the subdivision.

SKIP *(trying to appease her):* There, there, Angie. It'll be fine. I'll keep him out of your way. It's good of you to keep—

FLOYD *(loudly):* Rise up! Floyd's not stupid. Floyd's happy—ol' Floyd's *arisin'* with Jesus! Hey Angie, are you happy? Or stupid?

ANGELA: That's it! *(Picks up the phone)*

SKIP: What? What are you doing? He doesn't have anybody—nowhere to go—

ANGELA: I'm calling Social Services.

SKIP: Ange! Just one week. That's all. And, he's not well. You've heard his cough.

SOPHIE: Hey, Mom—

ANGELA: Quiet, Sophie. *(Listening for a response on the phone)*

*(*SKIP *sits dejectedly.* FLOYD *happily looks at his book, thumbing through the pages.)*

SOPHIE *(impatiently):* Mom!

ANGELA: What is it, honey?

SOPHIE: I want Mr. Floyd to stay. You and he believe the same. You have the same goal.

ANGELA *(shocked and disgusted):* What are you talking about?

SOPHIE: If you put down the phone, I'll tell you.

ANGELA: No. I won't put down the phone. Hello? Hello? Is this Social Services? I have a homeless man staying with me, and I would like to remove him. OK. *(Waits)* Hello? My name is Angela Wilkins. I have a homeless man staying here in my home. My brother brought him here from jail and I would like to have him removed. Yes. His name is Floyd, Floyd Carson. OK, I'll wait . . . What? It will take a week! That's impossible. I don't have that kind of—what? *(Dejected)* No, I don't want him to go back to jail. *(*SOPHIE *and* SKIP *give each other a "high-five.")* Thank you. Goodbye.

*(*ANGELA *slams the phone down.* SOPHIE, SKIP, *and* FLOYD *put on their "best" serious faces.)*

ANGELA *(looking at* SOPHIE *and* SKIP*):* Don't you even say a word. *(*SOPHIE *and* SKIP *try to hide their smirks.)*

(Phone rings)

ANGELA: Hello? Oh, hello, Mrs. Leavy. Yes. You're Sophie's Sunday School teacher. *(Pause)* You what? You want to come over today? Well, I'm afraid that wouldn't be poss—you're on the way over now? Oh. Heh . . . heh . . . no . . . um . . . that would be . . . be fine. Sure . . . We'll see you in . . . *fifteen* minutes? Sure. Bye. *(Yelling and motioning)* OK. Everyone start straightening up this place . . . *now!* Make sure Ol' what's-his-name is in his room.

FLOYD: That's Floyd, Angie, Floyd. Bye-bye. *(*SKIP *drags* FLOYD *offstage.)*

Scene 11

Setting: Angela's home the day before Easter

*(*SKIP, ANGELA, MAXINE, *and* AMBER *are seated in the living room.)*

MAXINE: Thanks so much for letting Amber and me come at the last minute. I really didn't think about it, but I guess if I were you, I'd be scrambling to pick up the house. *(Laughs.* AMBER *sheepishly laughs.)*

ANGELA: Oh, it's no problem. *(Glares at* SKIP *who is shaking his head.)*

SKIP *(sarcastically):* Don't worry, Mrs. Leavy. Angie's house was voted "First Runner Up" for a *Better Homes and Gardens* contest.

AMBER *(looking around, impressed):* Oh, really?

ANGELA *(smiling):* No. You know brothers. *(To* SKIP, *pulling him up.)* Don't you have to take the dog on a long walk?

SKIP: But you don't have a—

ANGELA *(pushing him out):* Have a great time, Skip. Give Scruffy a good workout!

SKIP: Scruffy? *(Exits)*

MAXINE: Angela, let me introduce you to Amber. She's Melissa's mom. *(*ANGELA *and* AMBER *say hello.)* Sophie told us you're coming to our special Easter program. We're so happy that you're going to be able to make it this year.

AMBER: Yes. We're thrilled that you're coming.

ANGELA *(incredulous):* Thrilled? My, my. That's the first time I've ever heard of anyone being thrilled about church. And I do feel honored that you want me to come so . . . so much. *(Tries to hide a little smirk)*

MAXINE *(knowingly):* Well, I know it must seem a little odd to you that these "church people" get so excited about so-called religion.

ANGELA: Well, I must confess that thought crossed my mind.

MAXINE: You know, I don't expect most people really to understand what we're talking about, but what we have is so much more than religion. It's a new life all based on what Jesus did on the cross for every one of us.

ANGELA *(getting slightly irritated):* I'm sorry. I hope I don't offend you with what I'm about to say, but I believe religion, or whatever you want to call it, is just an excuse to evade . . . life. I don't mean to brag, but I've come a long way in my life and have risen up and will continue to do so by my *own hard work.*

FLOYD *(calling out from the other room):* Hey. Rise up, Angie! *Rise up* with Jesus. Just like Ol' Floyd.

ANGELA *(embarrassed):* Oh, Floyd. I'm really sorry, um . . . my brother . . . uh . . . he asked me to . . . uh . . .

AMBER: We heard. That's great, Angela. Thank you so much. Floyd is so special. Our pastor has told us all about him.

ANGELA: Oh, yeah . . . Well, I'm only keeping him for a week. It's no big deal.

AMBER: Well, it's a great thing you're doing. Especially as a single mom myself, I know how hard it can be sometimes—

ANGELA: Yeah, well, I'm not licking my wounds. I'm rising up. I'm living proof of what hard work can do.

SOPHIE *(entering):* Mom. I was going to tell you that you and Floyd have the same motto.

ANGELA: Floyd? Me? Whatever could you mean, Sophie?

SOPHIE: Floyd says he's gonna rise, and *you* say you're gonna rise.

ANGELA *(clearly irritated):* Floyd has *nothing* to do with me. Hard work and success have nothing to do with the silly religious ramblings of a half-witted old man. Sophie, don't forget that while it's OK to have a little religion, it's hard work that leads to success. *(Gesturing around)* Just look around the house. All the nice things you see didn't get here by accident, you know. And since I just received a new promotion, we're moving to Delaware Park Estates! Just think, Sophie, we've come from having nothing to moving to the highest tax-bracket neighborhood.

SOPHIE *(muttering):* I'd rather be in our old house.

ANGELA: What did you say?

MAXINE: Angela, you've been so good to let us come. I brought Amber along to share her story. You two probably have a lot in common.

ANGELA: I don't really get what you mean.

AMBER: Well, like you, I'm raising a child by myself. My husband was a career military man. We'd been married for four years, and then we were stationed in Georgia. Soon afterwards our Melissa came along. But a week after she turned two. Dan was in a terrible accident out in the field. *(Hesitates, remembering)* He . . . ah . . . was very badly injured and didn't last the week.

ANGELA: I'm so sorry.

AMBER *(continuing):* Oh, I was devastated. For weeks I would just sit in the house and cry. Melissa and I came to stay here with my mother so Melissa could have some kind of order in her life. Meanwhile, I'd started taking pills and was totally out of it. Then one Saturday morning the doorbell rang. It was Maxine from next door. She brought a cake over to Mom and invited Missy and me to church.

MAXINE: And your mom.

AMBER *(smiling and looking at* MAXINE*):* Yes, Mom too. At first I wouldn't go, but I sent Missy to Sunday School. Then I noticed she was beginning to brighten up. She'd laugh once in a while, and she was so excited about going to church. I couldn't figure it out, so I just observed her for several weeks. Finally, I decided I would find out for myself, and I went to hear Pastor Barnes speak. He said God has an incredible love for us all, but our sin separates us from Him. I thought I didn't need to hear that.

ANGELA: Yeah, well, talking about sin is so . . . negative.

AMBER *(continuing):* But the good news was that God sent Jesus to die for me—personally. I never really heard it that way before. Then he said that Jesus arose from the grave on the third day. I always knew the story of Easter, but I never got what it meant.

ANGELA: What's that?

AMBER: It means that, by rising from the dead, Jesus not only took our penalty on the cross, but He defeated death! I really needed to hear that. Dan tried to tell me that. I wouldn't listen. Shortly after we moved to Georgia, Dan came home one day and told me he "got saved." I just laughed and thought he was on some kind of religious kick. But instead of wearing out, he became more devoted.

MAXINE: I wish I could have met him.

AMBER: Dan would tell me that some day he would rise just like Jesus did. He'd tell me "I'm going to rise!"

ANGELA *(to herself):* Oh, brother.

AMBER: I know he's in heaven now. I learned from Pastor Barnes that one day there will be a resurrection of all who trust Jesus as their Savior. That's my hope. Even now, it's still hard to think of Dan, and what happened . . . I miss him *so much.* But I trusted Christ to be my Savior. He's given me peace. It's still hard. I still struggle. But the greatest thing in my life is knowing Jesus. It's the greatest thing I have.

*__Choir:__ "Knowing You"

Scene 12

Setting: Later that evening in Angela's home

*(*SKIP *and* ANGELA *are seated, already in conversation.)*

ANGELA: . . . and then she told me that she knows Jesus personally. What a far-fetched notion. Ha! What she needs is to get a job. She needs to stop living in a fantasy world, and rise up out of that old neighborhood.

SKIP: Angela, there's more to life than money. You can be happy without—

ANGELA *(rising to her feet and raising her voice):* Don't tell me about happiness! Don't tell *me* how to be successful! After all the times I've bailed you out with my money—for which I've worked—

(Telephone rings)

ANGELA: Hello! *(Groans)* Oh, Priscilla.

(Lights come up on PRISCILLA.*)*

PRISCILLA: Why, hello, Angie-dear. I'm hearing that it's getting loud over there—pretty loud. Can I help?

ANGELA: Why no, *Prissy-dear,* I don't need your help.

PRISCILLA: Oh, Prissy! How *sweet.* You just feel free to call me Priscilla, honey. By the way, have I told you I had psychol—

ANGELA *(angry):* Yes, you did—several times! Do you know how you can do your Christian duty?

PRISCILLA: How, dear?

ANGELA: *By minding your own business! (Angrily hangs up)*

PRISCILLA *(quickly dialing and speaking to herself):* Oh, Flo, she's gone over the top! She called me "Prissy."

(Pause, lights down on PRISCILLA.*)*

SKIP *(to* ANGELA*):* You're still angry, aren't you?

ANGELA: Of course, I am! Nosy neighbors—loser brothers—half-wit boarders! Why shouldn't I be angry?

SKIP *(shaking his head):* No, it's not that, is it? It's still Tom. You can't handle him leaving you. Who are you more upset with—Tom or God?

ANGELA: *Be quiet!* You mind your own business, Skip Wilkins. Just mind your own business. *(Turns away, clearly hurting inside.* FLOYD *enters.)*

FLOYD: Ol' Floyd's gonna *rise! (Looks at* ANGELA.*)* Hey, lady!

*(*ANGELA *ignores him.)*

SKIP: Floyd, you'd better not talk right now. Angie's upset.

FLOYD: Oh, I know. Angie's stupid, not happy!

ANGELA *(points to the door):* Get out of here! *Both of you!*

SKIP: Let's go, Floyd. I think we need to take Scruffy for a walk.

FLOYD: Skip, Floyd is glad that you are happy. Now Angie is *not,* Angie is—

SKIP *(grabs* FLOYD *by the elbow and exits):* Come on, Floyd. Let's go.

*(*SOPHIE *enters.)*

SOPHIE: Hey, Mom. Where are Skip and Floyd going?

ANGELA: Don't ask. I'm not in the mood for talking right now.

(Doorbell rings; SOPHIE *answers the door, ushers* PASTOR BARNES *into the living room.)*

SOPHIE: Look, Mom, it's Pastor Barnes.

ANGELA *(looking away):* Tell him I'm—

SOPHIE: He's right here, Mom.

ANGELA *(surprised, collecting herself):* Oh. Oh, I'm sorry.

PASTOR BARNES: No, I'm sorry. I didn't mean to catch you at a bad time.

ANGELA: Well. It has been rather stressful lately. How may I help you?

PASTOR BARNES: I wanted to thank you for taking such good care of Floyd. We just found a place for him to live. I know it was a high maintenance situation for you.

ANGELA: Pastor, I don't mean to be disrespectful to you or your church people, but it seems to me that you're all avoiding reality.

PASTOR BARNES *(taken aback):* I'm sorry?

ANGELA: Everyone connected with you and the church talks about *(fingers making quote marks)* "knowing Jesus." What does that have to do with me, or anyone else who has been utterly burned by life? I wonder how much they know about what it feels like to be rejected. Do you know what that means? No. I'm afraid the only person I trust is Angela.

PASTOR BARNES: I'm so sorry, Angela. *(Chuckles)* I promise I'm not going to sermonize, but can I tell you a little story about our Floyd?

ANGELA: You mean your Floyd? Ha. What would *he* know about rejection?

PASTOR BARNES: Everything. If you've got a minute, I'd like to share his story with you.

ANGELA: Well, I don't know if—

SOPHIE: Mom! I want to hear it. Puh-lease! Pretty please with sugar on top?

PASTOR BARNES *(chuckles):* She did ask "with sugar on top."

ANGELA *(looks at her watch nervously):* OK. If it's not too long.

*(*ANGELA *and* PASTOR BARNES *sit down.* SOPHIE *remains standing.)*

PASTOR BARNES: Floyd was a lieutenant in the Vietnam conflict. He was a man who saw his fair share of combat—you know—the real ugly, close-up kind. One day Floyd's unit walked into a village that had been wiped out. There were no survivors in the whole place.

ANGELA: Oh . . .

PASTOR BARNES: Two days later, Floyd was point-man on a reconnaissance patrol in the jungle. He was walking ahead of his men when they were ambushed by the Vietcong. Floyd was the only survivor. For twelve hours he played dead. Eventually he was able to make his way back to his base camp.

SOPHIE: That's terribly sad.

ANGELA: Yeah.

PASTOR BARNES: When he returned to the States, instead of a hero's welcome, he and the other soldiers were met with jeers and boos by antiwar protestors. But what broke Floyd is finding out that his wife of five years had left him for another man. He was blindsided. The whole time he was in Vietnam, she had led him to believe she still cared for him. Floyd never recovered, and he fell into a life of drug and alcohol abuse.

ANGELA *(softly):* Oh, wow.

PASTOR BARNES: Floyd lost a lot of his mental abilities during those tough years of abusing the hard stuff and denying reality. His family was a very proud bunch and didn't want anything to do with a drug addict. So he had nowhere to go. He still wanders from time to time. The police eventually pick him up and put him in jail.

ANGELA: Oh. That explains how he met my brother.

PASTOR BARNES: One Thursday afternoon he stumbled into our church, a homeless and hungry wreck. My son was sitting on the front pew, reading a little picture booklet about Jesus when Floyd wandered in. My eleven-year-old Robby read it to him like one child to another.

SOPHIE: *Awesome*! I have that book. *(Goes out to get it)*

PASTOR BARNES *(continuing):* When Robby got to the part about Jesus' crucifixion and resurrection, something awakened inside Floyd, and he began to sob loudly. On hearing this, I ran from my office to meet Floyd. Well, to put it simply, Floyd trusted Christ that day. He *loves* that part about *rising up!* I'm sure the truth of the resurrection goes deeply with him after seeing all the death and suffering in Vietnam.

*(*FLOYD *and* SKIP *return.)*

FLOYD *(seeing* PASTOR BARNES*):* All right! It's Floyd's pastor-man! Happy Easter, Preacher!

PASTOR BARNES: Hey, Floyd. Happy Easter to you too! Don't forget the program tomorrow.

SKIP: Oh, we won't. We'll be there. We'll *all* be there! Right, Angela?

ANGELA *(sheepishly):* Right.

PASTOR BARNES: Floyd, I've got good news for you. Monday you'll have a new home. The Wallaces want you to live with them. They'll take good care of you.

FLOYD: Hey! Nice. Floyd likes the Wallaces. Floyd even likes Angie. Angie's mad all the time, though. Angie's got a load like Floyd did. Angie's OK.

*(*ANGELA *turns away, embarrassed,* SOPHIE *enters with a book.)*

SOPHIE: Mom! I've got the same book Floyd had. We got it in Sunday School a few years ago, and I've kept it on my bookshelf.

FLOYD: Hey! All right! Good book, Sophie. Good book! Lots of nice pictures.

PASTOR BARNES *(looking at his watch):* Uh, oh. I've gotta run. I have an appointment in ten minutes. I'll get back to you, Angela, about all the details of Floyd's move. I want to thank you again for being so good to Floyd.

ANGELA: No problem, Pastor Barnes. I'm glad to have done it.

PASTOR BARNES: Well, I'm out the door. Be sure to get to church early tomorrow. (Chuckles) All the backseats fill up fast. Bye.

FLOYD: See ya, Preacher.

(All say goodbye)

SOPHIE: Mom? Would you read my book? Pretty please? With sugar on top? *(Gives the book to* ANGELA.*)*

ANGELA: How can I resist sugar on top? Now—it's bedtime. You'd better wash up and hop in. I'll be up to tuck you in.

SKIP: I'm gonna get Floyd to bed early. I'm pretty tired too—from walking Scruffy. *(Winking at* ANGELA.*)*

ANGELA *(meekly):* Good night.

Scene 13

Setting: Angela's home later that night

*(*ANGELA *is seated in her easy chair next to the floor lamp. She picks up* SOPHIE'S *book.)*

ANGELA *(reading aloud):* Jesus was very kind. *(Haltingly)* He loved all the people. He healed their sickness and made them well . . . *(pauses reading and looks up, thinking, then resumes reading aloud, pausing periodically to reflect)*

He didn't ever do anything wrong. He never sinned. Later, all the people didn't like Him anymore. They nailed Him to a cross. They hurt Him, and He bled. Then He died. Jesus was . . . dead. After they took the cross down, they put Jesus' body in a cave and rolled a big stone in front of the cave's doorway . . . After three days there were some ladies who came to visit Jesus' body at the cave. But they didn't find Jesus there. Instead there were two shiny angels. The ladies were very afraid to see the angels, but one of the angels said, "Stop being scared. I know that you are looking for Jesus, but He is not here. He has risen up! Come and look at where the people laid Him. Don't you remember that Jesus told all of you before that He would rise up from the dead? Now go tell the others the good news!" *(Turns a few pages)*

Some people are mad at all the bad people that put Jesus on the cross. They do not understand that it was Jesus' Father, God, who put Him there. God put Jesus there to die for us. *We* are the bad people that put Jesus there. God put Jesus there to take our punishment so we don't have to be separated from Him forever . . . *(looking up, pensively)* . . . forever.

Before Jesus went to heaven, He promised to come back for all the people who trust in Him. There are many people who do not trust Him. They think they are not sinners. They trust in themselves. That is sad. Jesus said that He would come back for all the people who do trust in Him. They have their sins forgiven. Many who have died are in heaven with Jesus. When Jesus comes back, there will be a resurrection day. All the bodies of the believers will rise just like Jesus. The people that are alive will rise to meet Jesus in the air. All Jesus' believers will rise up.

(Thoughtfully) Rise up . . . I feel so ashamed. *(Looking up)* God, I've tried to make myself rise up by my own efforts. I've thought that good things and a great reputation could bring me a sense of importance and security. I don't know how to say this any other way than, I was wrong. Totally wrong. I was only kidding myself. God, I believe that you love me. I believe you sent Jesus to die for me, for my sinful heart. Please forgive me, and make me yours. Skip, Sophie, Amber, Floyd—they've all been trying to tell me in their own

ways how loving you are. Please include me with them. Be my Savior too. Amen.

Epilogue

SKIP *(to his "friend," the audience):* Ever since the day that Angie trusted Christ, she tells people she's rising to the top! *(Chuckles)* She still kinda gets a little frustrated when I tell her that she sounds just like Floyd. But then she laughs. I think she hugs Floyd every time she meets up with him. And they both say, *"We're risin' up!* Yeah, just like Jesus!"

***Choir:** "We Shall See Jesus" (reprise)

Information for Suggested Music

"Arise, Arise!" (Incorporating "Jesus Shall Reign" by Watts)
Words by Nancy Price and Don Besig
Music by Don Besig
Harold Flammer Music, a Division of Shawnee Press
P.O. Box 1250
Jay Park Plaza
9 Dartmouth Drive Bldg. 4
Marshalls Creek, PA 18335
www.ShawneePress.com

"At the Cross"
© 2004 Hope Publishing Company
Words by Isaac Watts
Music by Ralph Hudson
Choral setting by Joel Raney
Hope Publishing Company
Carol Stream, IL 60188
www.hopepublishing.com

"We Welcome Glad Easter"
© 2003 Shawnee Press
Susan Dengler
Shawnee Press, Inc.
P.O. Box 1250
Jay Park Plaza
9 Dartmouth Drive Bldg. 4
Marshalls Creek, PA 18335
www.ShawneePress.com

"We Shall See Jesus!"
© 1981 Homeward Bound Music/BMI
Arranged by Tom Fettke
Lillenas Publishing Company
Kansas City, MO 64141
www.lillenas.com

"Knowing You"
© 1994 and this Arr. 2004 Make Way Music
Words and Music by Graham Kendrick
Choral Setting by Lloyd Larson
Hope Publishing Company
Carol Stream, IL 60188
www.hopepublishing.com